CHRISTIAN
ART

Fresco, discovered at Dura, on the Euphrates, of the second half of the first century (Courtesy Oriental Institute of the University of Chicago). See page 20

CHRISTIAN ART

BY

C. R. MOREY

The Norton Library
W · W · NORTON & COMPANY · INC ·
NEW YORK

First Published in the Norton Library
1958
by arrangement with Liturgical Arts Society, Inc.
and Longmans, Green and Co.

W. W. Norton & Company, Inc., is also the publisher
of *The American Tradition in Literature*, edited by Sculley Bradley,
Richmond C. Beatty, and E. Hudson Long; *World Masterpieces*,
edited by Maynard Mack, Kenneth Douglas, Howard E. Hugo,
Bernard M. W. Knox, John C. McGalliard, P. M. Pasinetti, and
René Wellek; and other fine anthologies.

PRINTED IN THE UNITED STATES OF AMERICA

5 6 7 8 9 0

Table of Contents

Preface

THESE summaries of the five principal phases of Christian art were contributed as articles to *Liturgical Arts*. The absence of any survey of mediaeval art in English will perhaps be the best justification of their publication as a book.

The view here set forth of the Middle Ages and of the Renaissance that followed them may diminish for the reader the quaintness of the one and the glamor of the other. The writer hopes, in return, and in spite of the brevity of treatment, that there may result a juster picture of the mediaeval time as that which begot the modern realistic attitude and a more sober appreciation of the Renaissance as the *fons et origo* of many modern ills along with its indubitable contributions to progress.

There is a test of civilizations, or cultural epochs, well known and trusted by the historian of art. It is: what was produced by this or that race, or period, in architecture? Was the collective thought thereof sufficiently fresh, positive, and confident to produce in architecture a new and original style? It is worth pondering that, if exception be made of derivative manners, the two architectures of Europe which may without reservation be called original were produced by classic Greece and mediaeval France. They were thus produced because they were needed for the expression of two contrasting points of view, so different that the one could in no wise have originated from the other. The one viewed the world with the serenity of intellectual detachment, transforming experience instinctively into ideas. The other never extricated itself enough from circumstance to achieve the coolness of the Greek survey of life; seeking the concrete and the individual, it sought the infinite as well, not with calm logic but with the passionate intuition of faith. The one produced an architecture of reasoned simplicity, adhering to the horizontal, distrustful of unmeasured volume; the other built with complicated stresses and balances, with soaring vaults, and silhouettes that disappear in space.

The idealism of Greek art is quickly understood: it is indeed the uncanny lucidity of anything that is greatly Greek which stirs the beholder. The same Hellenic clarity possessed the Byzantine rendition of the Christian theme, enriched, but not obscured, by its sumptuous Oriental setting. But the realism of the Christian Romanesque and Gothic is more difficult to grasp, for it requires reflection and analysis to realize that the quest for the concrete involves the infinite. One cannot fix a point in space or in time or in the experience comprising both without using all infinity as a field of reference. The paradox of mediaeval thought and art is its simultaneous search for the particular and the universal; rooted to earth, the mediaeval soul aspired with unending confidence toward heaven.

These two modes of interpreting experience brought forth, by their collision, what was finest in the Renaissance, and they guide to-day the attack and defense of traditional positions. The same conflict affords a never-ending interest to the analysis of the Christian art of the Middle Ages. Christianity was the final expression of antiquity, and, since styles long outlive the content which inspires them, the artistic medium of Christian thought was for centuries what was left of the classic. When finally the mystic realism of the new faith broke the rational bounds of Greek idealism, the very effort involved therein imparted an ecstatic force to the Romanesque, and lives on in the energy of Gothic art, the most vital expression ever attained by Christian belief.

C. R. Morey

March, 1935

I

The Genesis of Christian Art

CHRISTIANITY has been so long a permanent factor of experience that it is difficult to imagine the time when it was not. Yet such a time there was; and once craftsmen essayed to paint, or carve, or build for the first time something that was to be Christian, with nothing to show them how it should look.

But around them lay the panorama of Hellenistic art, the cumulative result of the expansion, dilution, and adaptation of Greek architecture, sculpture, and painting. The earliest Christian craftsmen possessed, or were possessed by, habits of design and visualization rooted six centuries deep. Small wonder that the first works designed for Christian purposes have nothing Christian in their form or decoration.

The early Christian congregations met, like any new society, wherever meeting was possible: in the larger dwellings of the members of the community, or in a "hall" secured for the purpose. Later on, as church-building acquired self-consciousness and integration, we find survivals of these early expedients; the *atrium* of the house became the *paradisus*, the *parvis*, of the mediaeval cathedral; from the "hall," which in the Graeco-Roman language of the beginning of our era bore the name "basilica," came the name for the earliest and most important churches, and the inner disposition of nave and aisles.

The earliest of the Christian tombs that have survived to us—the subterranean chambers of the catacombs of Rome—

are decorated with the same kind of impressionistic vignette that one finds frescoed on the humbler walls of Pompeii, with subjects sometimes of naïvely pagan content. About 100 A.D. the Christian subjects commence: a Good Shepherd, adapted from Graeco-Roman renderings of Hermes or Aristaeus; an orant woman, belonging to the class of Hellenistic personifications and doubtless standing for the departed soul; and finally the first unmistakably Christian type—Daniel standing between his lions. The preponderance in catacomb frescoes of the second and third centuries of Old Testament figures and scenes over those of the New is very marked, but not at all surprising. The Old Testament had been translated into Alexandrian Greek long before the Christian era; its themes were known and its stories told in the Jewish colonies of every city of the Roman world. The New Testament was scarcely written when Christian art began; the figure of the Founder, clear in moral significance, was still obscure as a physical image; His deeds were still too variously recounted, and His sufferings too sacred, to become as yet themes for graphic representation. The idea that dominates the art of the catacombs, viz., deliverance from sin and death, could be and was at first embodied in the familiar stories of the Old Testament: Jonah made a satisfactory symbol of the Resurrection; Noah standing in his Ark (a mere box!) recalled the hope of salvation from the deluge of sin.

The miracles of the Saviour, guaranty of salvation, begin to appear in the catacomb frescoes of the second century, but only such miracles as the Multiplication of the Loaves and Fishes, or the Healing of the Paralytic, which could *omit* the Wonder-Worker; it sufficed the early believer that there be painted on his tomb the feasting multitude alone, in which he saw himself, symbolically, partaking of the sacrament which the scene connoted, or the paralytic walking away with his bed upon his back, as token of the Saviour's power that would be exerted for him as well as for the sick man of Bethesda. It is after 200 A.D. that, in those frescoes which can be identified with certainty as depicting the miracles, the figure of Christ appears—a youth of beardless face and short hair. It is in the third century that we find the first certain examples of the miracle of the Water Turned into Wine, of the Healing of the Blind Man, of the Leper, of the Woman with the Issue of Blood, in which may be seen this earliest artistic representation of Christ. He was also depicted as a beardless, short-haired youth at Alexandria, just as we see Him on a famous ivory box from that city, now in the Berlin Museum, seated among His disciples and teaching. Later the Alexandrian Church visualized Jesus, especially when performing His miracles, as carrying a short cross in the manner of a sceptre (page 73), and sometimes standing on the beasts of Psalm xc, like Horus on his crocodiles. In Asia Minor there was a variant of this youthful type which gave Him long hair flowing down upon His shoulders (page 79). From the second half of the fourth century the Asiatic East and Italy began to add the beard (page 75) that made from this type the head which has become traditional in Christian art.

There is still another reason why the Old Testament preceded the New in furnishing the themes of the nascent Christian art. It is becoming more and more evident that the early centuries of our era were familiar with *illustrated* copies of the books of the Old Testament, and that these

picture-books were first produced in Alexandria where the
first Greek version of the Old Testament was made. The
earliest books of this sort were of course in roll form, and
a copy of one of them, the famous *Rotulus of Joshua* (page
74), still exists in the Vatican Library. Before its parchment
membranes were detached from one another, the Rotulus
was thirty feet long, and bore an uninterrupted frieze of
drawings that told most of the story of the Hebrew conquest
of the Promised Land. The Hebrews in these drawings are
pictured as an army of Roman soldiers, and Joshua as their
imperator, all wearing costumes which are the same as those
of the soldiery depicted on the spiral reliefs of the Columns
of Trajan and of Marcus Aurelius in the second century.
The original from which the Rotulus was copied, directly
or through one or more other copies, cannot be dated later
than the Columns. The landscape background against which
the military scenes are enacted is indeed more akin to the
landscapes that one sees on the walls of Pompeii than the
landscapes of the reliefs on the Columns; it is composed of
mountain-ranges on the summits of which mountain-genii
recline, with here and there impressionistic, distant views of
cities, or groups of buildings, or gardens enclosing shrines.
To this early Alexandrian illustration of the Old Testament
can be traced all the early Christian illustrated books thereof
at present in existence, such as the Genesis of Vienna and
the remains of the Cotton Bible in the British Museum.
These Old Testament pictures performed a strange rôle in
mediaeval art: the Pompeian settings in which their scenes
were cast were preserved from century to century by the
persistent and faithful copying of the Alexandrian originals.
That is why we meet in Byzantine painting, far down in

the eleventh and twelfth centuries, those fresh landscape-vistas, Hellenistic-looking architecture, and the typical slopes of rocky hills that later made their way into Italian painting *via* Duccio and the Sienese, and still form the habitual background of the sacred episodes on Russian ikons. A singular case of the survival of early Old Testament illustration is furnished by the Genesis mosaics of the thirteenth century that decorate the vaults of the narthex of Saint Mark's at Venice; they were copied quite accurately, though with a certain Byzantine stiffness of style, from the illustrations of an Alexandrian Book of Genesis written and illustrated seven hundred years before.

The themes of the Old Testament, owing to this early standardization in Alexandria, became fairly well fixed in Christian art at an early date, and were apt to follow the same formulæ all over the Mediterranean world, wherever the prized Greek texts of the Septuagint, the Alexandrian version of the Old Testament, were used. Not so with the subjects of the New Testament. The different churches, Alexandrian, Syrian, Ephesian, African, Italian, Gallic, all had their own versions of the Gospels and their own images of the episodes narrated therein. A singular instance of this has recently emerged from A. M. Friend's investigation of the portraits of the Evangelists in the Greek and Latin Gospel-books. He has found that in Egypt the Evangelists were originally represented as standing figures, in Ephesus as philosophers seated in profile, in Italy as author-types sitting frontally, like the portrait of Virgil in a famous manuscript of that author in the Vatican Library.

The same local variation is found in the representation of incidents in the life of Christ. The Jesus who enters

Jerusalem in the early Christian art of Egypt rides over a rug which is spread in His path, while elsewhere in the Roman world a mantle takes its place. In Egypt representations of the Nativity were unique in including the curious figure of Salome, the midwife, who doubted the virginity of Mary and was punished by the withering of her hand, restored only after it had touched the swaddling clothes of the Infant. An angel accompanies the Magi as they approach the Christ Child in Egyptian Epiphanies; in Palestine the same is true, but the scene is symmetrical, with one Magus and the angel balancing two Magi on the other side of a frontally seated Virgin and Child. The very number of the Magi was still uncertain in the Christian art of the fourth century; a fresco in the Catacomb of Domitilla in Rome shows us four of them, and another of the third century in the Catacomb of SS. Peter and Marcellinus represents only two. The Annunciation was variously conceived; in Egypt the Virgin received the angelic salutation seated, while the Asiatic church conceived her as standing on that occasion. Christ seated on the globe of the world is a type found only in Latin works throughout the range of early Christian art; out of the Vision of Ezekiel the Eastern Church gradually evolved, instead, its own notion of Christ in Majesty, surrounded by a circular glory and seated either on a throne or on the arc of heaven.

Most interesting and puzzling of all the early modes of rendering sacred subjects are those that were in vogue, during the fifth and sixth centuries, in that belt of Latin culture which in late antiquity included northern Italy, distinguished from central and southern Italy, and spread across the southern part of Gaul into Spain. Here we find distinctive usages, ecclesiastic and liturgical, which once prevailed throughout the "belt," but which later were crowded out of Italy and Gaul into Spain and formed the basis of the constitution of the early mediaeval church in Spain and of its Mozarabic liturgy. In the period of which we speak, the south of Gaul and Spain were united in the Visigothic kingdom, and culturally at least allied with the north of Italy, newly important by reason of the transfer of the political capital of the peninsula from Rome to Ravenna. The individuality of this cultural belt is reflected in its ecclesiastic art. Here one finds, for example, our earliest existing representation of the Crucifixion (fifth century), depicting the Saviour nude save for the loincloth and differing widely from the extant Asiatic renderings, which come about a century later, wherein Christ is clothed in a long tunic. In our Latin school above mentioned we also discover that the lance-wound in the body of the Saviour was thought to be in His left side instead of His right, where it is put by the otherwise invariable rule of mediaeval art, and consequently in pictures or reliefs that represent the doubting Thomas approaching his Master, the disciple comes from the spectator's right, advancing to touch the wound in the Saviour's left side. In Italo-Gallic Baptisms of this school the Baptist is conceived as a shepherd and given a crook. Most curious of all is the manner of showing the Massacre of the Innocents, the slaughter of the children of Bethlehem, for in southern Gaul the soldiers do not stab the infants, but dash them to the ground—a distinction which is preserved in the Mozarabic liturgy when it marks the lesson for the day with the rubric: "in *allisione* infantium."

These Italo-Gallic peculiarities perpetuated themselves in

Western Europe in some cases far into the Middle Ages; Irish artists, for example, even as late as the ninth and tenth centuries, still sometimes place Longinus, the centurion who pierced the side of the Saviour, on His left. Carolingian miniaturists and ivory-carvers continue also another peculiarity of early Christian Latin iconography in picturing the Holy Sepulchre as a two-storied affair, a cubical lower portion supporting a rotunda. The origin of this notion is obscure, but it was undoubtedly helped by the existence of so many structures of this type in Provence, such as the tomb of the Julii at Saint-Rémy. The actual appearance of the Tomb of Christ as it looked *c.* 600 is preserved to us in the painted cover of a wooden box that was found among the relics of the Sancta Sanctorum at the Lateran in Rome, when its altar was opened in 1905. This box was filled with an amalgam of resin and sand in which were imbedded pieces of wood and stone picked up by some pilgrim to the holy places in or near Jerusalem at the end of the sixth century. The objects are all labeled with the names in Greek of the places from which they came, e.g., "from Bethlehem," "from the Mount of Olives," etc. The scenes painted on the cover have reference to some of these places; they show the Crucifixion, the Resurrection, the Ascension, the Nativity, and the Baptism. In the Resurrection we see the Sepulchre as a circular shrine with a conical roof and an altar in front of it, above all of which is poised the dome of the Anastasis, the church which Constantine built above the Tomb. The same picture of it appears on the little leaden phials in which pilgrims put the oil they took from the lamps that burned in front of the Tomb and the other *loca sancta*; some of these phials, dating also from the end of the sixth century, are still preserved in the treasury of the cathedral of Monza near Milan. In 614 the Persian Chosroes raided Jerusalem and destroyed the Sepulchre. Save for the obscure descriptions of early pilgrims, these phials and the painting on the lid of the reliquary box are our only record of the Holy Sepulchre as it appeared to visitors to the Holy City in the first Christian centuries.

The standardizing of the themes of the New Testament proceeded hand in hand with the standardizing of its text. Both processes were the result of the steady pressure of the Graeco-Asiatic church upon the rest of the Christian world. But the fact that the source of authority for Old Testament iconography was Alexandria, while that for the New Testament was Nearer Asia, produced a difference in the two sections of biblical illustration that was never completely obliterated, the one preserving its spatial background and picturesque landscape accessories, the other inclining more and more to a neutral setting for the Gospel episodes, which finally issued in the plain gold background of Byzantine mosaics.

Alexandria, in late antiquity, was the stronghold of what there was of realism, and of the realization of space, in Hellenistic art. The conceptions of the Alexandrian school are well reflected in the paintings of Pompeii; there we can see the freedom with which the movement and posture of the human figure were rendered, the expansiveness with which its surroundings were conceived, in short, the three-dimensionality of the world as viewed by these sophisticated artists, seeking, as metropolitan genius has ever sought, an escape to the "open spaces" from the complications and irritations of city life. In Greece and Asia, on the other hand, we find that the last phase of Hellenism takes a negative turn; evoking the past, it seeks by imitation to revive the glories of the Athenian art of the fourth and fifth centuries before our era. This classic style was two-dimensional, eschewing depth of background, and shutting in its space by an architectural treatment or by a sheer neutral wall (page 79).

There could be no question as to which of these two styles was to become the principal artistic vehicle of the new religion. Christian hope was fixed on the next world, not on this; its conceptions of ultimate reality transcended material experience. As the spiritual significance of the mysteries depicted was better understood, there was not felt the same need for minutely concrete representations, nor the same desire for that illusion of material existence which could be imparted by the Alexandrian indications of specific locality and time. The trend of Christian style was therefore in the main toward the two-dimensional, Neo-Attic wing of Graeco-Roman art.

The effect of this was at first to make it ugly. The antique ideal, the Greek quest, was one of material beauty, the presentation of life in typical completeness and perfection, but bounded by the bourne of the sensible world. The Christian painter and sculptor, child of centuries of Hellenic and Hellenistic naturalism, groped blindly through his inherited materialistic style toward an expression of his own immaterial concepts; it is no wonder that the early phases of Christian art destroyed the beauty of the past without achieving that of the future. Only in the sixth century do we find the new ideal successfully rendered in fitting form; in the mosaics and carved ornament of that period in Ravenna a

new principle of composition is visible which achieves unity
not through the traditional Greek insistence on a central
motif, but by rhythmic repetition of accents. If one compares
the processions of saints on the walls of S. Apollinare Nuovo
(page 78), or other mosaics at Ravenna, with any Greek
pedimental group, the new concept of unity emerges clearly.
The Greek effect is static; in the mosaics of the sixth
century the integrating principle is movement, conveyed by
a succession of color accents that perform the function of a
musical beat.

This change from the principle of balance and symmetry
to one of rhythm as the source of unity and beauty involved
the introduction of series and sequence and thereby of unlimited extent, albeit in the two dimensions of classic style.
The same revolt against the limitations of Greek unity was
accomplished in the architecture of late antiquity by the
introduction of the factor of space. Space is the element
whereby the interior of a building may be made to suggest
the romance of the unlimited, which the solids of the structure deny; its development in Christian architecture, like the
shift toward rhythmic composition in the representative arts,
measures the progress the new cult was making toward the
adequate expression of its spiritual content. Antiquity had
avoided the inclusion of space in architectural effect; the
classic example is the Egyptian pyramid with no interior
space at all. The Greek temple had used space, not indeed
for internal composition, which was the least of the classic
builder's preoccupations, but for the proper relief and isola-
tion of the colonnade of the porch. It is only in the Roman
phase of Hellenistic architecture, as in the Pantheon (page
76), that we find a building actually composed as an interior.

Even here the antique prejudice against the unlimited, the incommensurable, in short the infinite, toward which the Christian cult was oriented, produced a curious inhibition. The interior of the Pantheon is geometrically conceived, a half-sphere with no windows save the *oculus* in the top, promptly measured by the eye and therefore finite and controllable. In Hagia Sophia at Constantinople (page 17), built four centuries later, we see the same result, save that the geometry is more subtle, and the builders have done away with the carefully colonnaded walls and coffered ceiling which still in the Pantheon betokened the antique preoccupation with solids rather than voids. The supports are evasive, leaving somewhat the impression that the half-spheres and quarter-spheres of emptiness which the domes and semidomes inclose, are themselves the realities of the building, and the ceilings but their weightless definitions. But they are half-spheres and quarter-spheres none the less, commensurable and therefore not transcending the limits of experience. The Greek element in Byzantine art thus shows itself still strong enough to confine Christian concepts within the limits of a rationalized art.

The complete exploitation of interior space toward the Christian ideal of union of the finite with the infinite, of the interior with all of out-of-doors, was accomplished much later, in the Gothic cathedral, and lay at the end of a long evolution of Christian architecture in the Latin West. Nevertheless the germ of the cathedral and the statement of the space problem which it solved with so much beauty can be found in the early Latin basilica (page 77), at the beginning of the evolution. The very orientation of this structure shows the stirring of a new purpose. Antique buildings of

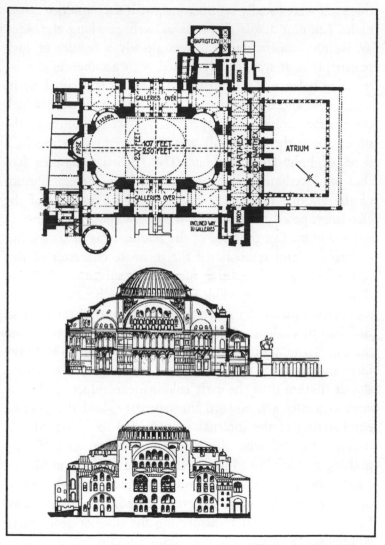

Ground plan, section, and side elevation of Hagia Sophia, Constantinople

this kind were usually symmetrical, with their interior colonnades running across the ends as well as along the sides. While the semicircular apse was already a feature of such pagan plans, it was usually paired with another in the interest of balance. The Christian interior was focused by its single apse and by the altar in the sanctuary, toward which the eye ran rapidly along the closely spaced columns of the nave; above the nave wall was the clerestory letting in a flood of light from without. The Christian basilica had thus produced an axis of movement within the equilibrium of the antique interior; it had also, in its opening of the clerestory, posed the problem of space without as related to space within. But the roof of the basilica was of wood, impermanent, and symbolic of the inchoate character of this unsatisfactory architectural form. The substitution of the Romanesque masonry vault for the Early Christian wooden roof responded hardly more to considerations of safety from fire than to aesthetic need. This vaulting of the nave started the Christian interior of the West toward its goal. The heavy piers and the wide bays of vaulted construction produced a slower rhythm than the early colonnade, conducting the eye with a greater awe toward the sanctuary; and the gradual emphasizing of the internal supports led to a vertical axis which competed with the antique horizontal axis. Finally nothing was left but to invent the ribbed vaulting of Gothic construction, that made the walls unnecessary and opened up the clerestory again, this time to admit a light transfigured by color, and transforming the interior from mere emptiness into mystically significant volume.

The early Latin churches arrest our attention therefore more for their implications of beauty desired than for their evidence of beauty accomplished. Hagia Sophia is witness to the crystallizing and rationalizing of the representations of Christian concepts in the Greek East at an early date; in the West these concepts integrated much more slowly, since the motive power in this evolution was far more emotional than intellectual. Latin art was therefore in the early Middle Ages less articulate than Greek, and for this very reason subservient to the more civilized formulæ purveyed by early Byzantine style. But these formulæ could not in the end satisfy the ecstatic piety of the West; the Byzantine is static in its ultimate effect like the classic, and the West was committed to an expansive style from the moment it conceived the apsidal orientation of its first churches. It is the intent and striving of early Christian art in the West that fascinates the student who studies its ugliness enough to understand it; in its impulses lies the genesis of the most expressive religious art that history knows, which came to full flower in the Gothic cathedrals a thousand years after the first Christians painted their obscure hopes on the walls of the catacombs in Rome.

II

Byzantine Art

*Byzantine art is not essentially different from that of
Hellas, which always took for theme the reality of
myth, in contrast to other arts, including that of our
own day, which pursue in vain the myth of reality.*
— Muratoff.

DURING the British Mesopotamian campaign of 1921, a
detachment of English soldiers occupying the promontory
of Salihiyeh on the west bank of the Euphrates stumbled
upon the remains of a little city, since identified as Dura.
This was, in ancient times, a Macedonian outpost established
to control traffic on the river, and, as Alexander's conquests
were stabilized, left there for the same purpose. It continued
to perform this function under Parthian and Roman rule.
Here was discovered a strange art, embodied in fresco and
gypsum reliefs, an art which was Hellenistic in its origins,
but shot through with Mesopotamian feeling. In the same
way the racial complexion of the region, to judge from the
names appearing in the inscriptions that have been discovered, gradually changed in the course of centuries from
Greek to Oriental.

The principal discovery at Dura was a frescoed wall with
a row of figures—two priests and the family of a certain
Conon for whom the work was done—dating from the second half of the first century A.D. Standing within an architectural frame, these resurrected personages stare out at the
spectator with the same frontality which stiffens the pose of
Greek saints in mosaics executed a thousand years later

(Frontispiece). The principle of rhythm in arrangement, the rich emotional play of color, has here orientalized Hellenistic style in quite the same fashion as in the mosaics of Ravenna, whose decorative quality in these respects was emphasized in the preceding chapter. It is no wonder that Dr. Breasted, the first archaeologist to examine and publish the frescoes of Dura, called them "Oriental forerunners of Byzantine painting."

They are, indeed, our earliest example of the transformation that Asia gradually brought about in Graeco-Roman art, a transformation whose early phase, as at Dura, was nothing more than the re-statement in Asiatic terms of Greek notions about the representation of nature. This transformation was later hastened by the fundamental shift of content in Near Eastern art from Greek naturalism to the immaterialism of Christianity. Because of its difficulty in understanding experience, the Asiatic mind, like the Egyptian, sought its ultimate realities outside of experience. The ancient arts of Pharaonic Egypt, of Mesopotamia, and of Persia all have this in common that, although they could *describe* facts and *narrate* occurrences, the facts were always isolated one from another, and the occurrences were always in mere sequence. The *relation* of facts to each other and the pregnant rendering of events, so as to suggest what preceded and followed —these are functions of the Greek intelligence. They were embodied in reliefs and paintings that arranged groups naturally in space, relieved the figure from its background, and made it a living whole. In Egyptian reliefs, the lack of such synthesis is so complete that there is not even integration of the human body: the head is shown in profile; the torso, frontal; the legs, in profile again. Occasionally one even finds an Egyptian figure with two right or two left hands.

The Greek, as it were, stepped back to get a proper perspective on life; the Oriental was too close to it to see it whole. The resulting fundamental difference between Greek style and the styles that preceded it was the Hellenic understanding of *spatial relation*. This understanding continued and was fully developed in the Hellenistic art of Alexandria, and was incorporated in the Christian editions of the Septuagint illustrated in that city, as mentioned in the preceding chapter; but the later Graeco-Roman style of Greece proper and of Asia Minor tended rather to restrict the depth of its compositions, to flatten its figures, and to limit its space. This tendency reinforced in the Hellenistic art of Asia Minor the traditional disposition of the Near East toward two-dimensional rendering, and toward the satisfaction of aesthetic design not in the illusion of material reality which continued to be sought in Alexandria, but in *pattern*.

As antiquity merged into the Middle Ages, and as the grip of Greek thought on Mediterranean culture was gradually loosened, such Oriental prepossessions regained their sway. Spatial relation in the representation of an event or object was replaced by unrelated narrative and description; the figures grew flatter; the background lost its depth and moved up into the forward plane; the old Hellenic triangle of composition, resulting from a unified arrangement around a central axis or motif, dissolved into a distribution of equal accents that determined a rectangle instead. By this process compositional unity tended to become rhythmic instead of architectonic; i.e., unity was achieved as in music by the regular recurrence of accent. The realism of local color that makes Hellenistic painting gay (and often garish) was gradually succeeded by a subtler choice of hues, departing more and more from the exact reproduction of local tones and tending more and more toward decorative harmony.

Such was the style that embodied Christian concepts in the decoration of the churches of Syria and Asia Minor in the sixth century—the product of a long process whereby the art of Graeco-Roman antiquity was denatured and sublimated to fit the requirements of the point of view of the Orient and of the new Oriental cult that had possessed the Roman world. We know the style best by the Gospel-Books illustrated in Asia Minor in the sixth century; one of these, the Gospel-Book of Rossano, furnished an illustration for the preceding chapter on the Genesis of Christian art (page 75). One may contrast this "Raising of Lazarus" with the picture also reproduced from the Rotulus of Joshua in the Vatican, representative of Alexandrian depth and freedom of composition (page 74). With this landscape the flat single plane of the Asiatic miniature is in sharp contrast, the latter even being unable to provide the space needed for the rear figures in its groups, whose heads appear to be stuck on the bodies in the forward register. Another specimen of Asiatic style, imported into Italy in the fifth and sixth centuries, was mentioned in the same chapter—a mosaic in S. Apollinare Nuovo, Ravenna, showing part of the procession of female saints who advance along the nave toward the enthroned Madonna (page 78). These figures have traveled far from Graeco-Roman nature; bodies are hard to imagine beneath their flat draperies; they cast no shadow; their stark fixation of the spectator's gaze turns them into ghostly symbols of themselves.

Revival of primitivism though this style may be, it had

two qualities that insured its popularity. One was its susceptibility to pattern, which means the distribution of motifs over a surface in a pleasing rhythm of accents. This made it far more successful as decoration than any Hellenistic style, since no penetrating depth could contradict or interrupt the surfaces and forms to which it was applied. Its other quality was the denial of material reality, which fitted it to the transcendental content required by Christianity. So completely did it satisfy the Asianized taste of the Mediterranean world in these respects that, at the end of the sixth century, it was on its way to conquer the whole of that world and certainly to become the official art of Constantinople, when an event occurred which profoundly altered the direction in which the Eastern Christian Church was going and that of its art as well.

This event was the Arab conquest of the seventh century. Within twenty years the followers of the Prophet, helped in their progress no doubt by the strong Monophysite leanings of the Christian populations of Upper Egypt and Syria and their consequent discontent with orthodox theology, lopped off from the Christian polity those foci from which the Oriental point of view was exerting most powerfully its influence toward the de-Hellenizing of Christian art. Deprived of its farther Eastern provinces, the Eastern Empire was reduced to its Hellenic patrimony of the Balkan peninsula and Asia Minor, and the Greek element in its culture was consequently strengthened.

As has already been pointed out, however, Alexandria, always at odds both in theology and art with her native neighbors farther up the Nile, remained an oasis of Hellenism in Egypt. In her ateliers there had grown up that

tradition of Bible illustration which maintained almost unimpaired the whole naturalistic paraphernalia of Hellenistic
style. But Alexandria was captured by Islam about 641 A.D.,
and the Persians had raided the city twenty-five years before. The emigration of the frightened populace which we
know commenced at the time of the Persian raid must have
assumed great proportions during and after the Arab assault.
Some of the unwilling exiles must have been Christian artists,
forced in the face of infidel dominion at home to seek their
living in the Christian cities of the Mediterranean. It is therefore no mere coincidence that soon after the capture of
Alexandria the wide area of Mediterranean art, which had
already been covered by the Asiatic style, begins to show
cases of Alexandrian Hellenism, intrusions of landscape and
lively humanity, which in one place may last only a generation or two, but in others takes root and grows, finally
to blend permanently with the Asiatic manner.

One of these naturalistic intrusions was revealed by Myr-
tilla Avery in her study of the frescoes of the church of S.
Maria Antiqua in the Roman Forum. Here from the sixth
century had been practised a wholly Asiatic style, quite
like that which we see in the sixth century mosaics of
Ravenna; but about the middle of the seventh century, this
is interrupted by a series of frescoes done by two or three
generations of artists of wholly different tradition. The
earliest of them at least, who label their works with Greek
inscriptions, replace the flat saints of their Italo-Asiatic
predecessors with others whose faces are modeled in the
beautiful Hellenistic manner of the best paintings of Pompeii and who have limbs and bodies that can still convey
their solidity through really functional drapery. One of

these painters has left us an unforgettable figure in the slim, wind-swept angel, legitimate descendant of the Victory of Samothrace, who stands before the Virgin Annunciate on one of the pillars of the choir. In the second generation, at the end of the century, Latin begins to mingle with Greek in the inscriptions, and the Greek fluency of the Alexandrian immigrants begins to yield to the old Asiatic stiffness. In the eighth century, Latin displaces Greek entirely, and only reminiscences of Alexandrian freshness are left amid the recrudescent Asiatic formulæ.

Then again at Salonica in 1927 a fall of plaster in the little church of Hosios David revealed a mosaic in its apse, showing Christ of the Vision of Ezekiel seated on the arc of Heaven, surrounded by the four mystic Beasts. Toward Him turn the figures of the prophets Ezekiel and Habakkuk. The Christ is beardless, like Alexandrian representations of the Saviour, and though Diehl and Xyngopoulos claim for the mosaic a date coeval with the church (the fifth century), the arc of Heaven never appears as the Saviour's throne in existing works of Christian art before the end of the sixth century. The Hellenistic vigor with which the composition is executed is to be attributed not to early date but to another of the Alexandrian exiles, who has further left his mark on the rocky mountain landscape behind the two prophets, with its distant views of architecture, the favorite setting of the Alexandrian illustrators of the Old Testament. In the same city the church of Saint Demetrius, which seems to have been decorated after a fire in the middle of the seventh century with a series of votive mosaics, reveals here and there in the series unexpected bits of the same sort of landscape.

At Constantinople the invasion from Alexandria had more

permanent consequences. We have evidence of the native
style of the capital, as reflected in the art of Asia Minor,
about the time when the dispersion of the Alexandrian
schools occurred, in the precious miniatures of a mutilated
Greek lectionary now in Leningrad (page 83). Here we find
the figures of the Rossano Gospel-Book again, but in larger
scale. There is the same absence of depth of background,
the same earnestness of gaze, the same narrative interest in
the episode, but the oddities that were aberrations from
Hellenistic style in the sixth century book have now become
stabilized as customary formulæ. The draperies and profiles
are without underlying structure, and the lines that indicate
detail in both are becoming stylized into patterns that will
emerge later as the hall-mark of mid-Byzantine design.

Against these miniatures we may set an Alexandrian example, one of the illustrations of the famous Psalter of the
Bibliothèque Nationale in Paris. There is good evidence to
show that these miniatures were done in Constantinople
in the seventh or early eighth century (the same date and
provenance that is assigned by its editors to the drawings
of the Rotulus of Joshua), and that the group who executed
the set was headed by an adept in Alexandrian style. The
David playing his lyre in the Pompeian landscape of the
miniature that we have chosen for illustration (page 82),
with Melody beside him and another personification emerg-
ing from behind the fountain to the right, is a creation of
poetry more Greek than Christian—a poetry less poignant
and personal than that which somehow informs the awk-
ward scenes of the Leningrad lectionary, and one that still
retains the Hellenic delight in mere objective beauty. Such
work is not native to Constantinople or Asia; the landscape

and the Greek grace of the figures reveal the hand of some emigrant from the metropolis of the Delta.

During the Iconoclastic Controversy that racked the Eastern Church from 728 to 842, ecclesiastical art languished, and tended to revert to its Asiatic past. But it did not disappear, and the monuments of church decoration and of manuscript illustration which remain to us from these troubled years are gradually becoming known. Italy, being in artistic style a province of Asia during this period, and at the same time free from the fury of the iconoclasts, furnishes us with mosaics and frescoes of the eighth and ninth centuries with which to bridge the iconoclastic gap. Such are the frescoes (page 80) adorning the walls of the church of S. Saba on the Aventine at Rome, where a band of Palestinian monks had founded a monastery. The scenes from Christ's life that appear here are singularly like the miniatures in the lectionary of Leningrad.

Iconoclasm had its real effect in Greece and Asia Minor; since ecclesiastics and donors opposed to images felt that they could properly replace with the Cross the paintings of Christ and the saints which to them were idolatrous, one result was a renewed popularity of the Cross as a decorative motif. A curious example of this practice was recently published by Meyer Riefstahl from the museum of Antalia in Asia Minor; a slab of marble carved with the figure of the Archangel Gabriel has on its back in inverse sense a cross; the slab was evidently turned round and upside down by some image-hater, who then had the cross carved on its visible reverse.

It is only at the end of the ninth century that East Christian artistic production resumed its accustomed volume, and began to feel again the charm of Alexandrian style. An early example of this resumption may be seen in the famous manuscript of the Homilies of Gregory of Nazianzus in the Bibliothèque Nationale at Paris. This book is profusely illustrated with miniatures representing all sorts of subjects, from the Life of Christ to the history of Julian the Apostate. They were done by more than one painter and in two styles that are easily distinguishable, one as a more advanced stage of the Asiatic manner and the other as the picturesque Alexandrian mode. The scenes from the Life of Christ adhere to the Asiatic tradition of their place of origin (page 84); the Old Testament stories have the lively movement and the mountainous landscape or perspective architecture characteristic of the illustration of the Septuagint (page 85). But it should be noted that the two styles are not combined in any one picture. In the Christ-scenes we find a Saviour who has increased in stature and dignity over the sometimes insignificant personage of the Leningrad lectionary, but the line of descent from such works and from such earlier prototypes as the Gospel-Book of Rossano is unmistakable. On other pages the background opens up into mountain passes or vistas enlivened with perspective architecture; the bodies move with free torsions; one sees fluttering drapery and a lively play of light and shade. Such pictures clearly derive their charm from the Hellenistic source of Byzantine style.

The difference between these Alexandrian miniatures of the Homilies of Gregory and those of the Paris Psalter is that the latter (at least the best of them) are actually in Alexandrian technique; the former are imitations. Where were the models for these imitations? The manuscript of the Homilies provides the answer; the book was written in Con-

stantinople for Basil 1 at the end of the ninth century, and
some of its miniatures are obvious adaptations from the pictures of the Paris Psalter or from a similar series. The work-
shop of such imitators was undoubtedly one of the great
imperial libraries of the capital; here were to be found illustrated Old Testaments imported from Alexandria, or pictures like those of the Psalter done in Constantinople itself
by refugees from the Islamic conquest of Egypt. Confronted
with such visions of recovered Hellenism, it is small wonder
that Graeco-Asiatic artists, no longer troubled by iconoclasm,
began to study and copy as best they could these formulæ of
Greek grace and beauty.

It was only in the tenth century, however, that the two
styles were finally fused, and it is therefore only from that
time on that one can use with exactitude the term "Byzantine" as applied to the art of the Eastern Church. For "Byzantine" means just that amalgamation of Oriental and Greek
which the collision of the two styles produced in Constantinople. The Asiatic element that dominated East Christian
art in the sixth century is relegated to the background; the
formulæ of movement and drapery are transmuted from
Asiatic angularity into Hellenistic grace. The frontal stare
of the sixth century is replaced by the favorite Alexandrian
three-quarter views of the head; it is hard to find in mid-
Byzantine art a face so severely frontal that it has not at
least some obliqueness of gaze. A landscape appears, stiffly
reminiscent of Pompeii. The composition returns to the
Greek triangle, arranging itself about a central motif. The
Oriental element, however, is still there, revealing itself in
the genius for rhythm and pattern, and the direct rendering
of the supernal content of Christianity. It is Oriental taste

that insists upon gold backgrounds for the Alexandrian figures in Byzantine mosaics and casts their forms in obvious
symmetry instead of the subtle balance characteristic of
Hellenic works. The high-lights that flash so brilliantly from
the mosaic walls of Saint Mark's or Monreale are what is
left of Hellenistic chiaroscuro, but it is Oriental genius
that turns them into rhythmic pattern, that transforms the
light-streaks into the gold lines of enamels and miniatures
and organizes these lines into decorative webbing. The
ascetic saints of the Asiatic style assume in the Byzantine
the authoritative pose and gesture of Hellenistic heroes, but
they are still set Orientally in two-dimensional space. Almost every individual motif of Byzantine ornament has a
Hellenistic source, but its ensembles are like nothing so
much as a Persian rug. The ornament and color—such
subtle color as no Hellenistic painter achieved—afford an
Oriental undertone to the theme that is carried by the figures, but this theme, in spite of its unreal content, is presented with a clarity that is altogether Greek.

It is the rising to the surface of the underlying decorative
feeling and its absorption of the figures to the detriment of
their dogmatic verity which constitutes the decadence of
this brilliant Byzantine fusion of Orient and Hellas. If one
compares the eleventh century Crucifixion at Daphni near
Athens (page 81) with Christ's Harrowing of Hell of the
twelfth in Saint Mark's (page 86), the difference is striking.
In the earlier work the decorative accompaniment is unob-
trusive, inherent in the creamy mass of the tragic figure on
the Cross, in the dull glow of the gold background, in the
reticent elegance of the sorrowing Mother and Disciple. In
the later, the movement has lost its rhythm in a medley of

diagonals which merely repeat the angular pattern of the high-lights of the drapery. The vitality which Greek tradition handed on to Byzantine, and which the mosaicist of Daphni knew how to transmute into spiritual instead of material being, is in Saint Mark's replaced by mechanical action. The eleventh century reduced the free movement of Alexandria to rhythm; in the decadence this rhythm became a mere succession of staccato beats.

Against this conventionalized art there arose a reaction, the full extent of which has only recently been realized, as the mosaics and frescoes of Serbia and Macedonia are becoming better known. The reaction was not toward the static dignity of the art of the tenth and eleventh centuries, but rather toward its fountain-head of Hellenism. "Neo-Hellenism," as this style of the thirteenth and fourteenth centuries has come to be called, aims at freedom of expression. The facial drawing becomes eccentric; the color forsakes the dominant gold-green-blue of Mid-Byzantine for a higher and wider gamut; the even rhythm of composition which keeps the earlier scenes so pregnant with spiritual sense is upset in the interest of dramatic episode. The influence of this movement was very great; it inspired the first essays of Russian native painting, and many believe that it lies back of the revival of painting in Italy. Its most brilliant monument is the mosaic cycle of the church of Kahrie-Djami in Constantinople, the only church of the great Christian capital that still retains its decoration. These mosaics (page 87) must be seen to be appreciated—in the real sense of this hackneyed *cliché*—for their color is their charm, and although it is here still disciplined by centuries of Byzantine taste, the palette shows as frank an enjoyment of hues for

their own sake as one might see in a wall-painting by
Pinturicchio.

After the fourteenth century Byzantine art is compara-
tively unproductive in its ancient habitats; its legacy passed
on to the Slavic art of the Balkans and Russia, and into
Armenian painting. In none of these provincial manifestations do we find again the delicate, satisfying balance of its
component factors that one discovers in the mosaics and
frescoes of the tenth and eleventh centuries. The one period
of startling achievement that Russian art enjoyed, in the
fifteenth and sixteenth centuries, was at a time when it was
least Byzantine; the refinement of the lovely ikons of this
period may be distantly due to Constantinople, but the
drawing has the *gaucherie*, and the color, the archaic force,
of the infancy of a new race.

Byzantine art, at its best, remains the finest expression
of Christian dogma that Christianity produced. It is, more-
over, not the mere letter of this dogma which its artists conveyed with such uncanny clarity, but its soul-stirring pro-
fundity. Nevertheless it is dogma, not faith, that furnishes
the theme of Byzantine art; the reason for the static perfection of its climactic period and its inability to evolve into
new forms of equal significance lies in just this Greek characteristic of intellectual rather than emotional apprehension
of the Creed.

III

The Romanesque

THE development of the Romanesque style in Christian art parallels in the West that of the Byzantine style in the East. Both resulted from the penetration into Graeco-Roman-Christian art of ideas external to the Hellenistic culture of the Mediterranean basin. In the East, Byzantine art arose from the effect of Semitic and Iranian culture upon the Hellenistic tradition—a tradition which was sufficiently native and strong to sustain this influence without essential impairment. In the West, where Greek civilization existed only in a secondary, Latin form, it met with a more violent barbarian invasion which ultimately engulfed it, despite the naïve effort of the barbarian races themselves to revive the Rome which their fathers had ruined. We call that the Romanesque art which reflects the gradual sinking of Latin culture below the Celtic and Teutonic surface.

One must remember the varying degree in which Western Europe had been Latinized by the time the Western Empire fell. Italy, the Midi, and Spain were almost as Roman as Rome herself, dotted as they were with cities where urban life went on in a mode scarcely distinguishable from that of the capital. But the north of France and the Rhenish, British, and Danubian frontiers, lacking the frequent towns of the South that might have served as foci of Latinity, had been far less penetrated by Latin culture. Beyond these frontiers were the Celtic and Teutonic tribes, hostile by tradition to all things Roman, and as yet un-taught in the new faith, which provided within the decaying Empire, against all forces of disintegration, at least a common mode of thought.

Yet in this uncharted limbo beyond the frontiers lay the germs of a new art, whose curious opposition to the principles of the Hellenistic and Byzantine can be detected in native Celtic and Germanic work before the latter knew the discipline of Graeco-Roman style. An initial of the Book of Kells (page 89), a product of eighth or ninth century Ireland, will illustrate such barbarian art in nearly native purity. There is no denying the unity, or, therefore, the beauty, of this initial. But it is a unity that is not built up around a central axis after the manner of the Greek triangle; nor yet does it depend upon a regular recurrence of accents, as in the rhythmic composition of Ravennate mosaics. The letter has unity because it *lives*; its coiling vitality makes symmetry or rhythm unnecessary. We are confronted with a design that needs no further guarantee of power to please than the conviction it imparts of organic life. Beside the Greek mode of architectonic (built-up) composition and beside the Oriental rhythm, we must place this third means of achieving unity, which we may call variously dynamic, or realistic, but which we must at any rate recognize as un-Latin and barbarian.

Such composition unconsciously seeks out the asymmetric and eccentric effects of nature itself; and the result of its first collision with Latin style was to throw the latter out of balance. We see this clearly in the early mediaeval work of the south—in Italy, south Gaul, and Spain—where the barbarian infiltration was not strong enough to give a new and positive orientation to artistic style, and hence acted as an additional factor of decay. An example of such disturbance of classic equilibrium are the towers that spring up early in the Middle Ages to qualify the symmetrical silhouette of basilican churches (page 88). One can trace the growing sense of instability in the coarsening of ornament, its gradual loss of precision, its increased irregularity of drawing (page 98). One of the surest signs of the mediaevalizing of Latin style is the diminution of weight in the carved or painted human figure; the attitudes are unbalanced, the feet dangle, the gestures lack conviction, and the draperies flutter unreasonably. An ivory book-cover in the Bodleian Library at Oxford (page 91) is singularly illustrative of this loss of plasticity: in some of its scenes it is an eighth-century copy from a late antique plaque executed in the south of France or the north of Italy of which part survives in the Berlin Museum and the rest in the Louvre (page 90). The fifth-century figures of the Berlin ivory are remote enough from the nobility of classic style, but they at least have weight and solidity of construction; the mediaeval copy makes them dangle and topple like puppets on a string. The extreme of this denaturing process is to be found in Spain, where craftsmen in their renderings of the human figure sank to the lowest terms of primitive design.

In the north of France, in that area bounded by the Seine, the Rhine, and the sea, where nearly all the creations of the Middle Ages originated, from the vast concept of the Holy Roman Empire to Gothic architecture, the Teutonic settlers were numerous enough to leaven the lump, and their effect on the moribund Latin style which they absorbed with their first lessons in Christianity was surprisingly galvanic. We cannot enter here into the obscure stages by which Teutonic realism found its way to expression by means of the symbolic themes which it inherited from antique Christianity. It will suffice to acquaint the reader with the earliest example we have of this transformation of antique Christian style, an example that is without doubt one of the masterpieces of the whole history of art.

It is an illustrated Psalter[1] now preserved in the library of the University of Utrecht. The authors of the line-drawings (page 92) which illustrate not only every psalm, but also ten canticles, the Te Deum, the Gloria in Excelsis, the Lord's Prayer, the Apostles' Creed, and the Athanasian Creed, are unknown, but we do know that they lived and worked in some monastery in or near Rheims. Lately Dimitris Tselos has shown that they used for model a Latin text illustrated after the Greek fashion of Alexandria, or else a text that had copied the pictures of such a Greek Psalter. Certainly the mountain landscape of the Alexandrian Septuagint illustrations is as much to the fore in the Utrecht Psalter as in the Rotulus of Joshua, and other reminiscences of this ancient Greek tradition are present in the foreshortened buildings nestling in the hills and shaded by trees. But instead of the impersonal characters of Hellenistic art, we find on these pages a throng of intense individuals—figures that twist and lunge and gesture in an extreme of excitement. For the first time in the history of European art, the artist *feels* and is thrilled by the content of the scene he is depicting; his very literalness shows how specifically he sees the actions suggested by the psalter's text, and how strongly he realizes the emotions of the persons whom he makes to

[1] A facsimile of the miniatures of this Psalter has been published recently by the Princeton University Press.

enact the scenes. The realistic attitude is here fully apparent for the first time, and with it that romantic *ambiente* which always accompanies a convincing rendering of the concrete.

The influence of this manuscript was enormous. It was taken to England some time between *c.* 850 and 1000 and copied twice; in English work of the eleventh century there are many reminiscences of its drawings. On the continent we find echoes of its extensive repertory of motifs—a veritable mine for any copyist—throughout the range of Carolingian art. In fact the school of Rheims can be, without much exaggeration, considered the fountain-head of all that was creative and progressive in Romanesque style. Its sketchy, nervous pen-work passed into England to be developed at Winchester into figures of larger scale (page 93) with formulæ of drapery and pose that are but conventionalizations of the free expressiveness of Rheims. This northern drawing makes the figures float like the unstable beings that one encounters in the early mediaeval work of the south; both are Romanesque in the volatility that comes from an emotional rather than an intellectual content. But the emotional element in southern drawing only makes it weak; in the north the young Teutonic spirit galvanized the antique forms into significant activity. The vividness of this expressionism was too strong for painting; it found its medium rather in an outline drawing which has no moments of hesitation or rest.

In the course of the twelfth century in England, the fluent style hardened into a bold, curvilinear manner of remarkable power. On the continent, the Carolingian renaissance of the ninth century had hardly passed before there came a reaction toward a less volatile rendering of the figure and a more plastic style. One can trace this reaction by the ivory plaques that were carved at Saint-Denis and Metz down to the end of the tenth century, at which time the tendency to substitute form for line began to localize itself along the Rhine, and finally became the gospel of that school which dominated German art from the end of the tenth century— the school which developed in the monasteries on the island of Reichenau in Lake Constance. From about the year 1000, in fact, the political division of northern Europe between France and Germany is reflected as well in its Christian art: to the west of a line drawn through the Rhone, the Saône, and the Meuse, one finds in both north France and England a pervasive lyric quality which retains the windy line of Rheims, while to the east, in the Rhineland and even so far as Saxony and the Upper Danube, there is a steady trend toward closed contours, more reticence in pose and gesture, and greater solidity of form.

Bishop Bernward of Hildesheim in Saxony visited Italy in the year 1001, and lived for a time in the palace of the Emperor Otto iii on the Aventine of Rome, near the church of Santa Sabina. This church boasts a pair of wooden doors executed in the fifth century, carved with scenes from the Old and the New Testament. Bernward must have studied them with interest, for when he returned to Hildesheim he organized a school of bronze-founders who made for him the famous doors (page 97) of the cathedral of Hildesheim (they were made originally for the church of Saint Michael) with reliefs depicting scenes from the Old and New Testament, as at Santa Sabina. He may have meant to rival the Roman doors, but the style of which his craftsmen made use has nothing Early Christian about it, being rather a translation into bronze of the wide-flung, excited action that one sees in the pages of the Utrecht Psalter. At Rome the Bishop saw also the Columns of Trajan and of Marcus Aurelius, and determined that if the deeds of Roman emperors were given such honor, Christ's deeds should receive no less; so his craftsmen were also called upon to make a bronze Easter column to serve as holder for the paschal candle, on which in winding spiral strips that imitate the ascending friezes of the columns of Rome, is depicted the life of Our Lord from His Baptism to the Entry into Jerusalem. Contrasting with the doors, the reliefs show the characteristic German tendency away from the lyric movement of Rheims, and toward plasticity; the groups are massed, the figures are of heavier and more solid scale. In spite, however, of heavier proportions and greater restraint, the Teutonic realistic genius still shows itself in bursts of impulsive action, beak-like and expressive profiles, heads thrust forward truculently, and bodies whose vigor pushes them through the clinging drapery.

The theory of the Holy Roman Empire which viewed Italy as an imperial province was firmly held in the eleventh and twelfth centuries, and toward 1100 it bore singular fruit in the migration of this plastic, German version of Rheims style into Lombardy, reviving in the peninsula after many centuries a truly sculptural tradition to replace the flat, denatured carving into which Italian sculpture had sunk (page 98). The authors of this revival occasionally signed their works, and the signatures reveal Germanic names; the head and founder of the Lombard school signs himself *Wiligelmus*, and has left a principal record of his crude but powerful style in some reliefs on the cathedral of Modena (page 96). Wiligelmus and his followers, restorers of monumental

mass and authority to sculpture in stone, gave vogue to such
decoration in Italian churches elsewhere, and the propaga-
tion of their style can be traced beyond the Alps into France
and Spain; in Catalonia the word *Lombardo* came to mean
a stone-mason.

West of our dividing line of Rhone-Saône-Meuse, the lyric
mode of Rheims persisted. Taking root in England, it informed the vigorous line of manuscript miniatures produced
in the monasteries of Winchester and Canterbury. The su-
periority of English drawing in the tenth, eleventh, and
twelfth centuries was well recognized on the continent; we
have record of the admiration caused by an illuminated English manuscript that was passed around a provincial council
at Limoges in the eleventh century, and some of the most
prized manuscripts of the library of the monastery of Fleury
on the Loire were gifts from English scriptoria. At any
rate, from about 1000 A.D. on into the twelfth century, there
is a steady infiltration of this lively style, giving free vent
to the emotional piety which pervaded pre-Gothic Christianity, through the north of France and into Burgundy, and
later into the valley of the Loire and the Midi, until we find
it finally even replacing the decadent Latin tradition in
Spain. At the end of the eleventh century there appears in
Spain and Languedoc a style of monumental sculpture based
on this tradition of ecstatic line, which constitutes the
strangest mode of carving stone in the whole history of sculpture (page 94). One can understand it only by remembering
that the dominant graphic art of the earlier Middle Ages
was the illustration of manuscripts, and that the cartoons
from which these sculptors worked came from monastic
scriptoria. The effort of the sculptors of Languedoc was

therefore to recapture in stone, by dint of undercutting and sacrifice of mass to swirling line, the religious levitation of the draughtsman. Such art has the same ardent and wholly irrational inspiration as made the First Crusade.

The story of Romanesque architecture is in essentials the same as that which we have traced in painting and sculpture. The legacy of Roman building descended to the Middle Ages by no means unimpaired; the highly developed technique of throwing level concrete cross-vaults across huge spaces was lost by the sixth century, even in the East, where the architects of Hagia Sophia resorted to domical vaults and domes to cover their interiors. When the basilican churches of Italy had to be rebuilt, they usually showed, as at Saint Clement's in Rome, a shrinkage in size. Yet there was always in early mediaeval building the same intent to be as Roman as possible that we find in the other arts, with the limitation that the Rome which the Middle Ages remembered was the city and empire of Justinian rather than that of Augustus, or Trajan. Charlemagne, when planning his imperial chapel at Aachen, took for model the sixth-century church of San Vitale at Ravenna, and even in the eleventh century Saint-Front at Perigueux is ultimately based on Justinian's Church of the Holy Apostles at Constantinople.

The Romanesque style developed into something un-Roman through no desire of the builders to depart from the Roman tradition, but because of structural and liturgical necessities, and also because of the unconscious growth, beneath its conscious reverence for the antique, of a Teutonic aesthetic. The Latin basilica, roofed with stone or brick vaults instead of wood, became the Romanesque cathedral

or abbey-church, with its style departing from the Early
Christian norm only in proportion to its distance from Rome
itself (page 95). In the City, the early Christian basilica was
maintained, wooden ceiling and all, throughout the Romanesque period, and the same is true very generally throughout the peninsula, until the introduction of vaulting from
the north. But in France, where Romanesque architecture
had its fullest development, the old basilican type steadily
changed in two senses with the advent of vaulting. In the
southern sunshine, light was sacrificed in order to make the
side-aisles high enough to buttress the vaulting of the nave,
eliminating the clerestory. In Provence the vaults of aisles
and nave were simple tunnels; in Perigord domes were
used; in Poitou, cross-vaults; but in all these southern schools
the side-aisles lift their ceilings to the vaulting of the nave.
In the north, the necessity of light made the clerestory the
main *desideratum*; the solutions range from the simple ac-
ceptance of the wooden roofing for the nave, as at Vignory,
to the daring height of Burgundian naves, raised high above
the side-aisles to admit the clerestory lighting, and depend-
ing on massive walls and accurate construction for their
stability. The final solution, timidly attempted first in north
Italy, of arching the ceiling vaults on an armature of stone
ribs that carries the thrust to the main supports of the structure, was finally worked out in Normandy and the Ile-de-
France, where also the builders slowly realized the consequent superfluousness of the intervening walls and began
to open up the whole clerestory with windows.

When this point was reached, Romanesque was turning
into Gothic. It had traveled, in other respects as well, a long
way from the Early Christian prototype. The quick suc-

cession of columns that carry the eye in an Early Christian interior so rapidly to the apse was replaced, as vaulting replaced the wooden roof, with a sparser series of piers; the rhythm became slower, and the approach to the altar was charged with a constantly increasing significance. The antique horizontal axis began to turn, with the accentuation of the piers, into a vertical one. The necessary massiveness of vaulted construction, and the dimness of interior lighting in a building where large windows were always a risk, contributed to the ever deepening Romanesque effect of emotional rather than rational apprehension of the Creed, of intuitive and ecstatic grasp of a content which the mind could only view as mystery. Thus does Romanesque architecture furnish the romantic counterpart of that realistic strain which the Teutonic imagination injected into mediaeval Christianity and its art; the remoteness of this attitude from the clear Hellenic view, and from the scientific rationalism of the present day, is what imparts to Romanesque interiors their air of mysterious antiquity.

IV

Gothic Style

IN THE last analysis, style is the imprint on artistic expression of a point of view, be it the point of view of an individual, an epoch, or a race.

In Europe there have been but two points of view of sufficient general validity to produce that greatest expression of a collective consciousness, namely, an original style of architecture. These have been the Greek and the Gothic; and we shall better arrive at an understanding of the Gothic point of view, and thereby of Gothic style, if we compare the Gothic manner of regarding the world with that which informed the masterpieces of classic art.

The Greek point of view was one that felt *clarity* to be the supreme necessity. In order to achieve a bright clearness in this world, the Greek delimited it, including within its bounds nothing that transcended human understanding. To make it clearer still, he intellectualized it, transforming with uncanny ease the facts of experience into ideas, and individual objects into types. The Greek was a materialist, since the unknown, the unlimited, the infinite, being beyond the intellect to conceive, did not for him exist. He was at the same time an idealist, in the sense that he cared little for the particular save as a step to the general. The world of fact, for the Greek, was unconsciously and instantaneously transformed into intellectual concepts of universal truth.

Hence the orderly composition of Greek works of art, like facts marshaled in the mind. Hence the distaste in Greek relief for any indefinite extension, either of the third dimension into depth, or of breadth, or of height; the outer figures of a group in a Greek relief turn inward, and the background is neutral. In Greek architecture we find a resolute emphasis of solid over void, since the solid has form that can be defined, while space connotes the unlimited and the inexact.

Opposed to this materialistic idealism of the Greeks, which dominated the ancient world from the time it achieved integration in the fifth century B.C., is Gothic realism. A realist finds difficulty in understanding the quick Hellenic transformation of experience into idea. He lingers more lovingly on the particular; ideas to him are cold things. If he lingers too long, and sees no more in a landscape or a human individual than what greets and charms his eye, then he is no realist, but a naturalist. The realist is one who grips the concrete, but at the same time by intuition grasps the universal significance that it implies. Thus realism involves not merely the quest of the particular, but also that of the universal; and yet the universal is not conceived ideally as a defined type, but as something unknown, uncharted, romantically extended, of bounds indefinite and remote. The infinite that lurks about the particular is most readily apprehended in painting, for here no particular object can be depicted, in any specific space and time, without the implication of that unlimited space and time which is necessary to its complete reality.

It was the realism innate in mediaeval architects that urged them toward the Gothic style. The Gothic in all its manifestations takes its rise in the north of France, and it was here that architects first raised the Romanesque vault in order to free the clerestory for the admission of the light that connoted unlimited space. Here it was that the ribbed vault was developed, which made the whole structure into an armature of stone, whose interstices could be filled with windows. We, too, seek light and space, being realists as well as they. But the infinite to them was God, and the light that connoted it was of divine emission, so that they instinctively gave it that spiritual and poetic content afforded by the color of their windows. Viollet-le-Duc tells us of first seeing, in his childhood, the windows of Notre Dame at the moment when the organ burst into music, and child-like, thinking that "the windows were singing." Gothic windows indeed transform daylight into a hymn of color, while a modern window admits it as raw material. Theirs is a mystic realism; ours a material one.

The characteristic composition of realism is eccentric. Nature is never symmetrical in the particular, and only becomes so as we organize her into ideas. Hence the irregularities in Gothic superstructure, the unexpected variety in the ceiling vaults, the unsymmetrical façades. The vagaries of Gothic plans are famous. Plans drawn to scale of *portions* of Gothic buildings have been found, which had been inscribed on the smooth surfaces of blocks while they were lying in the workshops, but we have no authentic example of a complete drawing for a cathedral. The detail of each part was separately worked out, and one portion joined to another.

The cathedral thus grew, sometimes for a hundred or more years, and it seldom concealed the *gaucherie* of its infancy. As new ideas in vaulting developed, they were put into practice, often without changing the older vaults to make them match. The simile of a tree's growth is irresistible, and has often been used to illustrate the coming into being of a Gothic structure; and the branching ribs of a Gothic nave have often called up the image of a wooded aisle in a forest.

The Gothic structure is in fact organic, when compared to the dead weight of post and lintel that constitutes the principle of Greek building. Each rib has its function in the stability of the structure, a stability maintained like that of a living thing by balance of stress and the meeting of thrust with counter support. The evolution of Gothic piers and ribs in France may be traced by their attenuation as the builders reduced their diameter more and more in adjustment to the task each had to perform. Where new functions emerged, as at the string-course of the nave, or where the vaulting ribs began to branch in the base of the clerestory, there is a burst of leaves and flowers (page 101), as if the builder wished at these points to emphasize the vital adequacy of his organism.

Such Gothic ornament is Nature itself. The old Roman vocabulary of ornament, used for so many centuries by the Romanesque builders, disappeared, and in its place came the flora of France. The earliest capitals have budding leaves that are as yet not unfolded; as the style develops, the leaves expand, and in later phases they have an over-maturity and dry expansion that connotes an autumnal decline. The genius of Gothic is seen in nothing so much as this employment of local flowers and plants for ornament, without conventionalization—a phenomenon of realism in sharp contrast to the stylization of natural forms that was learned by the Greeks from Egypt, and by them taught to all the decorators of antiquity.

The cathedral dominates French Gothic style. Everything in Gothic art is in some way connected with it, from the illuminated books used for its services to the sculpture that adorned its walls. The cathedral itself is the expression of that understanding of the world which the twelfth and thirteenth centuries believed they had achieved. It is as much an exposition of mediaeval Christianity as the *Summa* of Thomas Aquinas. And like the theologian, it finds an ultimate harmony out of infinite variety; its thousands of statues, windows, grotesques, and reliefs are brought to final unity by sheer soaring faith. The complexity of the world and the intricate adjustments by which it is ordered, from the Gothic viewpoint of realism, make strange contrast with the serene simplicity of a Parthenon, complete expression of the Greek notion of experience, wherein no individual eccentricity is allowed to ruffle the calm surface of the ideal. The Greek theme is, as it were, played on a flute; in Gothic there is orchestration.

The sense of the infinite invests each Gothic phenomenon. One feels it not only in the opening up of the interior space into communion with the infinite reaches thereof connoted by the colored light. It is present also in the interior space itself, undefined in contrast to the geometric domes of Roman architecture, losing itself in the shadowy severies of the vaulting (page 99), and broken up by the piers and arches so that its extent is eccentric and uncharted like the green vistas of a forest. But on the exterior too we find the same courting of the infinite (page 100); the pinnacles that taper to the sky, the crockets on every straight line that break its continuity into dissolving points, the ever-increasing complexity of the tracery—all show a compelling desire to dis-

solve the forms and solids into the surrounding space, which
is the expression of the Gothic yearning for union with God.
If one compares an early façade like that of Paris with
Amiens and again with Rheims (page 102), one can see the
steady advance of this Gothic trend; at Paris the buttresses
are still dividing the façade into three separate portions,
and the structural members and solid walls are still evident;
at Amiens the buttresses disappear in their lower portions
behind a screen of statues, the portals heighten, and acquire
a perforated gable that masks the west wall; at Rheims the
lunettes of the portals disappear, and the whole west front
dissolves in an intricate design of tracery and colonnetted
galleries.

To test our characterization of Gothic realism, we may
turn from the macrocosm of the cathedral to the microcosm
of the illuminated manuscript. It is the habit of this art
to accept the ultimate significance and beauty of all things,
and particularly to admit the lower forms of nature which
Greek art excluded or threw out of focus in its glorification
of man. The Gothic realist was a master of detail, as he
must needs be who senses the infinite in the particular.
The pages of Gothic manuscripts, like the carvings of the
cathedrals, are thus filled with all sorts of beasts and birds
and flowers that have no function of illustration of the text.
The Romanesque predecessors of the Gothic illuminators,
impregnated with the pessimism of dying antiquity, had
looked on nature as a filthy thing; the Gothic artist saw it
as beautiful in ensemble and in detail, and crowded every
bit of it that was possible into whatever he carved or painted.

His script is made up of the same crockets, dissolving
letters into points, that served the stone-masons of the ca-

thedral to satisfy their craving for disappearing form. His
initials have the eccentric composition and carelessness of
symmetry that mark the plan and superstructure of the cathedral; as they progress in style, they shoot a sudden branch
to the bottom of the page, and this, a generation later, begins to sprout ivy-leaves and to grow, until in the fourteenth
century it has become a border of ivy-vine extending all
around the page (pages 107-110). In this convenient arbor
perch the members of the Gothic menagerie—real and fan-
tastic animals and birds, creatures human and half-human,
disporting themselves in mock-combats or the chase, and
sometimes being a parody, like an ironic foot-note, of the
sacred scene enacted in the miniature-panel at the top.

In one page here reproduced (page 109) the panel above
the initial represents a cathedral or abbey-church. The architectural element is always prominent in Gothic illumination
in the thirteenth century; it is as if this art instinctively felt
in the cathedral a sort of cosmos in which it had its place
and whose ultimate unity would justify its vagaries, and
give them spiritual substance and meaning. The little
churchmen in the scene here depicted are youthful despite
their tonsured heads; this is an art of youth like the Greek
art with which we have compared it. In all the history of
European style, these two phases stand out as ones in which
the prevailing ideal is one of youth, and the prevailing note
is one of optimism. Both embody the sense of having solved
the riddle of existence—the Greek with his ideal material-
ism, the thirteenth century Frenchman with his mystic and
delicate adjustment of the material and the divine. Both de-
pict mankind as young and cheerful; and both maintained
the illusion not more than a century or two.

Gothic art is in its first phase the art of the cathedral; a decline ensued when cathedrals were no longer built. As the art "comes down from the cathedral," to use Réau's expressive phrase, it loses its significance; the youthful optimism becomes a simpering mannerism; the statues that once played their part in the symbolic complex of the cathedral become artificial in pose and gesture now that their *raison d'être* is gone (page 105). The art resorts to superficialities—the multiplication of folds of drapery, the tilting of eyes and brows, the thrusting out of the hip and cocking of the head. The structure of the body, which had no interest to the symbolic craftsmen of the cathedral, is unknown, since there was no tradition for its study. Gothic style in its interest in the infinite had not sufficiently analyzed the concrete.

Thus ended the French phase of Gothic style, which dominated Europe through the thirteenth and the first half of the fourteenth century even as Greek style once dominated the Mediterranean. The shifting of emphasis from the universal to the particular, or, shall we say, from the cathedral to the easel-picture, took the leadership in Gothic art from French hands and gave it to Flanders on the one hand and to Italy on the other. In the Adoration of the Lamb (page 106) one can, with some trouble, discern the *disiecta membra* of the symbolic machine of the cathedral, but obscured behind a preoccupation with concrete fact. Hubert van Eyck in planning this picture showed himself the inheritor of the great iconographic tradition of French Gothic art, but his younger brother was the one that painted the stark nakedness of the Adam and Eve and lingered with meticulous fascination over the brocades of the music-making angels.

The rise of the easel-picture marks the rise of the individual. Made by a single artist for a single patron, it concerns itself with the individual point of view of the one or the other. The fourteenth century was the century of the Babylonian Captivity and the gilded slavery of the Popes at Avignon; the authority of the Church on which men had once leaned was gone. Communion with God was no longer convincing through the aisles and windows of the church; it must henceforth be vouchsafed the individual soul by its own levitation. Hence the importance of the individual in the religious art of the fifteenth century, and not only of him, but of the material environment whereby his individuality was defined; as interest in this develops, religious significance is blurred, and the fifteenth century, in the north and to a large extent in Italy also, was given over to naturalism. Details of interiors—furniture, stuffs, still life —are depicted with an analysis that obscures the human actors; even saints and Divine Persons are thrown out of focus by this indiscriminate recording of material fact.

Yet, in the midst of this obscuring of the imaginative side of realism by an apparent surrender to the merely natural, there emerges, in Gothic painting at least, the unmistakable quest of the infinite as well. The unlimited effect of space that once was afforded by the soaring interiors and vast windows of the cathedral reappears in the distant landscapes of the altar-pieces. The neutral backgrounds that sufficed for the symbolic compositions of the earlier style are pierced to give the vista into the unknown which, to the realistic view-point, is indispensable. The spiritual effect of these vistas is most apparent in Memling's pictures; place a card over the landscape of Martin Nieuwenhoven's Ma-

donna (page 104) and see how much the Virgin loses of
suggestive power. Or compare with the paintings of the
Netherlandish painters the similar compositions of the German Gothic carvers of religious reliefs; the latter seem merely
quaint to us, lacking the unlimited background that gives a
universal validity to the paintings, though the same homely
and concrete human beings enact the sacred story in both.

In Italy the substitute for the cathedral was found in a
different way, and in one characteristic of its classic tradition. Here the deeper implication of realism was rendered
not by the landscape background, but by significant form.
The prestige of French Gothic was strong in the Italy of the
Trecento, when Italian Gothic flowered; France was the
arbitrix elegantiarum of Europe in that time no less than it
is to-day. Giovanni Pisano and his fellows (page 103) followed therefore the French formulæ, even in the decadent
forms which by this time they had assumed; the Madonnas
are hipshot and the draperies complicated into flowing lines
of artificial grace. But beneath them the form expands, to
invest them with a new significance; pose and gesture become motivated by a content that is deep and true, instead
of an aesthetic ideal of aristocratic elegance. The Madonna
turns her head sharply to the Child, and the Child in turn
gazes fixedly into His Mother's eyes as if to surprise in them
the secret of His Calvary. The playful formulæ of French
Gothic style, invented to embroider a complicated symbolic
system, have suddenly become tragic. Into the single figures
of the Italian sculptors and painters of the fourteenth century is poured the whole theme that once was rendered with
bewildering variety and complicated harmony by the sculpture, glass, and structural intricacy of the cathedral.

Gothic style is thus the expression of a realistic point of view. Its history may be divided into three phases: (1) a phase that may be called the French phase, or the cathedral phase, or the mystic and ideal phase; (2) a decadence of the foregoing; (3) a phase to be known as Gothic realism, or the period of the easel-picture, or the epoch of the individual. The first phase is one in which the innate love of the concrete facts of nature is controlled in the interest of a symbolic portrayal of the Christian conception of the world as the reflection and creature of God; in this period it finds its full realization only in the ensemble of the cathedral, and satisfies its craving for the infinite that complements the particular in the sense of unlimited space engendered by the cathedral's undefined interior and its colored windows. Deprived of the cathedral's unifying function in the fourteenth century, the style decays in French hands, to be regenerated as its underlying naturalism is revived in Flemish painting, wherein the emphasis shifts from a collective and congregational point of view to that of the individual, and from a symbolic setting for natural objects to a real one. But this real setting itself reintroduces the infinite in the unlimited backgrounds of landscape, and thus hands on to modern art its chief avenue to communion with the unknown. In Italy the universal significance connoted more vaguely by the Northern landscape is packed, after the classic manner, into the single figure, illustrating a law of the history of art that Italy, when stimulated, will react in antique fashion. The emphasis on form that Italian art thus manifests, even in its Gothic period, was destined to become its shibboleth in the late fifteenth and in the sixteenth centuries, and ultimately to delude Italy with the notion that it could profitably ex-

change its native Christian art for an imitation of that of
Greece and Rome. When the classic revival of the sixteenth
century ensued, to spread itself in succeeding centuries over
the rest of Europe and ultimately to invade our own shores,
Gothic art was submerged. It throws some light on the history of European and American culture in the period since
1500 to remember that with the giving up of Gothic style,
Europe also surrendered its native point of view, and adopted
one that was exotic to it, and that has never ceased to trouble
it, and America as well, from that day forward.

V

The Renaissance and Christian Art

THE RENAISSANCE presents a different aspect each time that definition of it shifts its angle of approach. To some it is the resurrection of antiquity, the "revival of learning"; to others the advent of humanism, the reassertion, as opposed to the humble concept thereof conveyed by mediaeval teaching, of individual importance. In both of these conceptions, the Renaissance is something new, something that arose in Italy, something that originated in the late fourteenth and early fifteenth centuries.

The historian of Christian art would nevertheless insist that what was new in the Renaissance was not invented till the sixteenth century. The naturalism of the fourteenth and fifteenth centuries is to him quite as Gothic a phenomenon as the cathedral art of the thirteenth—even more so, since its revelation of the absorbing beauty and interest of man's environment, and its analysis of individual character in man himself, is only the emancipation of the innate realism of Gothic art, which had been till the fourteenth century controlled by the symbolic synthesis of scholasticism. The mediaeval church had transformed Gothic delight in nature into love of God, but when this focal tension was relaxed, it was not surprising that nature became as fascinating as its Creator. And if one seeks to identify specifically the spot in Europe where this expansion of Gothic realism began, priority is to be assigned not to Italy, but rather to North France and Flanders, always the breeding-ground of mediaeval change. Transferred to Italy, the realistic movement took on more striking aspect in the very degree to which the freer personality of the Italian artist could detach itself from the collective tradition of the Middle Ages—and also took on more loveliness, by virtue of Florentine grace and sensibility to form. The Italian also wakened sooner to the beauty of antique architecture and sculpture, but only to grace therewith the realistic world that the North had discovered before him. Italian art of the fifteenth century is still at core as Gothic as that across the Alps, however much of its outward aspect and embroidery may be reminiscent of antiquity. Like the *palazzi* of its architects, the façade delightfully translates the Roman into local dialect, but the building stands by virtue of the Gothic vaulting within.

The fifteenth century is thus the flowering of that realism which was the vital element in Gothic art. Its interest in humanity is part and parcel of the fresh enjoyment of a material world, whose beauty must no longer be viewed as either meretricious or symbolic. The very wonder with which the early humanists received the revelation of ancient lore, the romance that surrounded their search for manuscripts, the Christian virtue which they ascribed to antique philosophizing—all this bespeaks the continuing humility of the mediaeval mind. But mediaeval above all is the catholicity of both the art and scholarship of the Quattrocento; from the wealth which antiquity unfolded and from the entrancing variety of the material world, there was no attempt to select the beautiful and perfect as distinguished from the merely interesting. Scholars delighted in anything they could dig up of ancient literature, and had not yet become the pedantic critics of Latin texts and style which they were in the succeeding centuries; in painting and relief, the classic reminiscence is part of an indiscriminate accumulation of detail—a welcome addition to the minutiæ of backgrounds and interiors and to the *genre* by-play which has so dispersive an effect upon Quattrocento composition and testifies to the unselective curiosity of the age.

The pictures of Filippo Lippi (page 113) are perhaps as good examples as one can find in Italy of such wholesale recapturing of nature. The same absorption in the physical world, to the prejudice of religious content, can be found across the Alps in the painting of the Van Eycks (page 111) and their followers, the difference being that the northerner is mainly entranced by his physical environment, the Italian by human grace and charm. But neither is consciously forsaking the ways of his mediaeval forbears; the naturalism of both has no conscious intent beyond the service of the Church. These painters of the fifteenth century were painting in normal fashion, i.e., seeking to portray experience as they and their epoch understood it, and if they, with no un-Christian purpose, made man and his surroundings more interesting than God, they were no less thereby the true exponents of their time.

But the sixteenth century presents us with a new repertory, filled with the personnel and paraphernalia of antique mythology. The Italian Quattrocento, which delighted in Roman ornament and *putti* to relieve the homeliness of its faithful rendition of Quattrocento life, and dressed its gods and goddesses in contemporary clothes, was followed by an age which could and did evoke antiquity with archaeological exactitude. Sansovino's Bacchus (page 114) might pass for a real antique. Indeed one feels the Olympian presence even in the Christian subjects of the sixteenth century, and divines an Apollo tortured by the arrows of Saint Sebastian, a Juno enthroned in the Madonna's place (page 112).

These Italian sculptors and painters, or the patrons for whom they worked, had not of a sudden become Greeks and ancient Romans. But there had come about a curious revolution in artistic thinking and practice, the counterpart of similar thinking and doing in the fields of politics and religion. This revolution may be described as the emergence of the academic point of view, or, perhaps more effectively, as the divorce of beauty from truth. It resulted at any rate in the notion of an absolute standard of perfection, achieved merely by taking thought, and without necessary relation to past or present experience. This is the new thing presented by the Renaissance to the western world, which has never since ceased to labor with the difficulty of relating the resultant ideal of unity—submission of parts to the whole, conformity to type—to its traditional Gothic and realistic habit of particularity and diversity. The Quattrocento had discovered and employed the antique as a picturesque embroidery; the Cinquecento enthroned its forms and style as an infallible norm which human behavior must be made to fit. The early humanism had recognized in ancient literature and art no more than a sympathetic expression of its recovered sense of human dignity; the Cinquecento saw in the antique a perfection which could be regained by mere exercise of logic and convenient ignoring of contemporary fact and past tradition.

The political applications of this academic way of achieving order are evident through the sixteenth and seventeenth centuries, most conspicuously in the arbitrary partition of

Italy by Charles v in 1530, and in the centralization of France under the Bourbons, when city charters, feudal rights, and the privileges of guilds were submerged in the quest for unity and uniformity. The Council of Trent, in its effort to purge the mediaeval church of its abuses, pursued the same ideal of *a priori* perfection, and, in its effort to eradicate the mediaeval weeds, killed many a tradition that was healthily rooted in local practice. There is no doubt that the religious conflict helped along the academic point of view in both the Protestant and Catholic camps; both sides were conscious, if Europe was not to fall into religious chaos, of the necessity of uniformity of belief; and on both sides this zeal for unity outran its objective. The excesses of the Inquisition and the Index were of wider effect but of no different quality from Calvin's tyranny at Geneva.

One single obscure effort was made by Gothic style to embody the new desideratum of order and unity in its own language. French writers call it the *Détente*; its examples are few, and were executed in the centre and east of France in the early sixteenth century. One of these is the female saint (page 118) in the Princeton Museum, a statue that has all the feminine nobility which a Greek presentment could give, and is classic also in its self-completeness. But it is also Gothic in every affectionately handled detail, and realistic in the best and ultimate sense because it reveals through its lovely homeliness the fundamentals of human character and emotion.

The uniform pathos which the sculpture of the *Détente* exhibits is suited to the melancholy passing of Gothic tradition in Christian art which was witnessed in the sixteenth century. The same tragedy, at the same time, was enacted

in the work of Michelangelo, a truly religious soul, who by
sheer genius forced the dying Gothic content through the
medium of classic form. His powerful, inhibited figures re-
flect the disparity between Christian emotion and the antique ideal (page 116), between free human will and the
Will of God. The rational forms of classic sculpture were
not made for the ecstasy of a Christian mystic; they writhe
in the possession of an unfamiliar spirit, and betray by brutal
distortion, incongruous proportions, and discordant composition the force of the collision of mediaeval Christianity
with the Renaissance.

The problem that tortured Michelangelo's genius, with
results of tragic beauty, was solved by the Baroque, albeit
by removing the factor therein of the individual soul. A
style of Italian origin, but of European range, the Baroque
reflects that aristocratic internationalism which spread over
Europe in the seventeenth century, as the ruling classes divorced themselves from contact with the people, convinced
themselves at length that they alone constituted society, and
felt in consequence their membership in an international
polity. The old Gothic attachment to local and individual
peculiarity, the rooting of religion in personal experience,
the consequent sincerity which still survives all classic training in the work of Michelangelo, were obstacles to formal
grace and elegance which the Baroque ignored.

In the fifteenth century, composition was still Gothic in
its promiscuity; the sixteenth was in nothing so classic as in
its insistence on the architectonic building-up of its ensembles, with a dominant central focus which restored to composition the long-lost Hellenic triangle. The Baroque,
however, tended rather toward a diagonal axis, seeking the

soaring and disappearing effect of flame (page 117). W. F. Stohlman, in his lectures on Renaissance and modern sculpture, defines the effect of Baroque as "the movement of mass *in space*." The last phrase is essential to the definition, since otherwise the Christian art of the seventeenth century, in its essential of unifying movement, would coincide with that produced by the second school of Pergamon, and represented by the frieze of the Great Altar at Berlin, and the Laocoön of the Vatican. The difference lies in the self-containedness of the Hellenistic figures; any one of the gods or giants of the Pergamene frieze makes a satisfactory composition in itself, since its movement, however violent, returns upon itself by *contrapposto*. Baroque figures on the other hand court the space about them, reach out to it like licking tongues of fire, and soar within it (page 117). Baroque churches, however much they follow classic rules in orders, domes, and centralized plan, nevertheless contrive to expand the limited interior of the Pantheon into spatial suggestion of unlimited extent (page 120). This suggestion, the introduction into ideal concepts of the notion of infinitude, is, as was pointed out in what was said of Gothic style, an element of aesthetic effect entirely un-classic, but thoroughly Gothic and Christian. Thus was the Baroque enabled, like Michelangelo, to bend the Hellenic vocabulary of academic art to Christian expression, disturbing by movement its classic calm, merging the feeling thereby generated in a space charged with the Divine Presence, illimitable and undefined.

But unlike those of Michelangelo's art, Baroque effects are not poignant; the fervor which inspires its tumultuous movement is sincere enough, but it is not the fervor of the individual soul. The Baroque is an art of a Papacy without local attachment, whose territory was the world; it is the expression of the international Society of Jesus, an art of kings by divine but not popular right—the first style, in fact, in the history of art to which no local or racial adjective can be fittingly attached. It is also an art, for all its emotional volume, whose genesis is academic and intellectual; its far-flung compositions, the spacious vistas of its interiors, the apparent freedom of movement in its figures and architectural forms, are in the last analysis as carefully controlled and planned for decorative propriety as any ensemble of the sixteenth century.

It follows that Baroque achievement, lacking concrete focus, is more original and valid in the abstract media of architecture and music than in the arts that reproduce nature. The interiors of Jesuit churches revive the infinities of the cathedral, though with disciplined and academic elegance. In music the Baroque period was creative enough to produce a new form—the opera—yet here again an ultimate academic inspiration can be divined in the assumption that dramatic action is capable of reduction to rhythm.

Nevertheless it was not the Baroque, but its French counterpart in the Bourbon seventeenth century, that established in Europe and handed on to our own times the academic point of view. The Bourbon method of transforming France, Gothically diverse in the political and religious sense, into the marvelously homogeneous nation that we know today, was not a frontal attack upon the mediaeval institutions, but an undermining competition. Thus the military establishments of feudalism faded away as their uselessness was demonstrated by the new institution of the standing army; free thought and expression at the University dwindled in view of the new prosperity of the royal Collège de France. So also the guilds, which maintained the Gothic tradition of native French art, deprived of royal and aristocratic patronage by the establishment of the Academy of painting and sculpture, disappear after the seventeenth century.

Following royal and aristocratic taste, the Academy and its branch in Rome, which it founded as a training school for young French architects, painters, and sculptors, had nothing but contempt for native style. The Bourbon state, as organized by Richelieu and Mazarin, needed for its success just those principles of abstract logic and centripetal unity which were the outward aspects, but not the inner well-spring, of Hellenic culture. The last Valois kings of the sixteenth century had already accustomed the ruling class in France to classicism as interpreted by the Italian Renaissance, though with an admixture of traditional style which resulted in the charming synthesis of native and antique which one admires in the chateaux of Francis I and Henry II, and the painting and sculpture of Fontainebleau. But with the development of the Bourbon régime there come a more knowing application of Vitruvian rules and a closer imitation of Roman marbles, which make the seventeenth century resemble in its archaeological correctness the Italian Cinquecento. The playwrights of the time are perhaps the best exponents of such neo-classicism in the pains they took to fit romantic action and personality into the unities and types of Greek drama. The movement and *brio* of the Baroque, and above all its reintroduction in academic guise of Gothic space, were thus reduced or excluded from Bourbon official art by the rigidity of academic rules. The single

Baroque sculptor in France in the seventeenth century was Pierre Puget, and he had small success at Versailles. Baroque architecture was largely confined to the churches of the French Jesuits, which themselves are commonly more sober in effect than their sister churches in Italy.

The Baroque of Italy is better termed an official and ecclesiastic art than a Christian; of the style of Versailles, even when it turns to Christian subjects, it is hard to use the word "Christian" at all, so deeply are the artists steeped in pagan lore and pagan style (page 115). The same applies to the adaptations elsewhere in Europe of both Baroque and the French Academic: in Germany, the Low Countries, and England. Quite different is the "Baroque" of Spain. Here is seen for one thing a continuation even into the seventeenth century of mediaeval native woodcarving, accentuated and realistic polychroming, and Gothic multitudinous detail. Nor do the sculpture and painting of Spanish churches, for all their adopted Italian classicism, ever follow Italy into the generalization of the grand style, nor France into barren academicism. The content of the Spanish Baroque is concretely and poignantly sincere, as might be expected from a race whose Christianity, even to the eve of the sixteenth century, was a militant faith, crusading against an infidel frontier. The seriousness and surviving realism of the Spanish art of the Renaissance are evident in an outstanding quality that distinguishes it from the Renaissance in France and Italy: the Spaniard never shrinks from *gaucherie*, or a sacrifice of formal beauty, to clarify and enforce a Christian theme.

In Pedro de Mena's "Saint Francis" (page 119) one might say that the Christian art of Europe came to an end. Here, in this singularly modern-looking figure, there is still pure Christian content, and a technique whose sophistication does not mask its Gothic derivation. But although, since the Baroque period, there have been countless churches built, and statues carved and pictures painted for their adornment, the architecture, sculpture, and painting which have been thus employed were not Christian in origin or *raison d'être*. The academic point of view demoted the intuitive and instinctive in art, whereby in the Middle Ages Christianity's grand theme had found naïve but real expression, and established in its stead the principle of beauty achieved by theory and rules, capable of transmission by pedagogy, and subservient to the absolute and exotic standard of classical antiquity. Thus was artistic perfection divorced from experience, religious or otherwise, and reduced in scale to the intellectual possibilities of its creator. The academic styles that have succeeded each other since the seventeenth century, as a consequence of this curious divorce of beauty from truth, can hardly be classified as Christian art, since they recognize no inspiration higher than the human mind.

Index

Acknowledgments: The author and publishers wish to acknowledge their gratitude for the illustrations on pages 73-120. The following plates are from publications: 74 (Biblioteca Vaticana, il Rotulo di Gíosuè); 75 (Muñov, il Codice . . . Rossano); 80 (P. Styger in Römische Quartalschrift, 1914); 82, 84, 85 (H. Omont, Facsimilés des Miniatures des plus anciens manuscrits grecs de la Bibliothèque Nationale); 89 (Sullivan, Book of Kells); 92 (Dewald, Illustrations of the Utrecht Psaltar); 93, 109 (Herbert, Illuminated Manuscripts). For the following plates thanks are due to: 83, the Frick Art Reference Library; 107, the Pierpont Morgan Library; 76, Kennedy and Company, New York; 83, 94, 95, 99, 101, 102, 115, Les Archives Photographiques; 73, 77, 78, 79, 81, 86, 88, 96, 103, 105, 111, 112, 113, 114, 116, 117, Alinari; 90, Giraudon; 100, 104, 108, the University Prints, Newton, Massachusetts; 119, Stoedtner; 120, Anderson.

Ivory book cover at Ravenna; carved in Egypt in the sixth or seventh century and depicting four miracles of Our Lord, the Three Hebrews in the Furnace, and the story of Jonah (Page 7)

A portion of the Rotulus of Joshua: Joshua is twice represented, standing and kneeling to the Angel of the Lord before the city of Jericho (Pages 8 and 23)

Miniature of the Rossano Gospels, from Asia Minor, showing an early bearded Christ in the scene of the Raising of Lazarus (Pages 7 and 23)

The Pantheon at Rome: first building to be composed as an interior, from an engraving by

The early Christian Basilica: interior of S. Apollinare in Classe, Ravenna (Page 16)

Sarcophagus of Graeco-Asiatic workmanship in Ravenna: Our Lord, the Apostles Peter and Paul, and other saints (Pages 7 and 14)

Christ healing the paralytic at the Pool of Bethesda: fresco of the eighth century in S. Saba, Rome (Page 78)

The Crucifixion: mosaic of the end of the eleventh century, at Daphni, near Athens (Page 31)

David the Musician: miniature executed about 700 A.D. at Constantinople, incorporated in a Greek psalter of the tenth century in the Bibliothèque Nationale at Paris (Page 27)

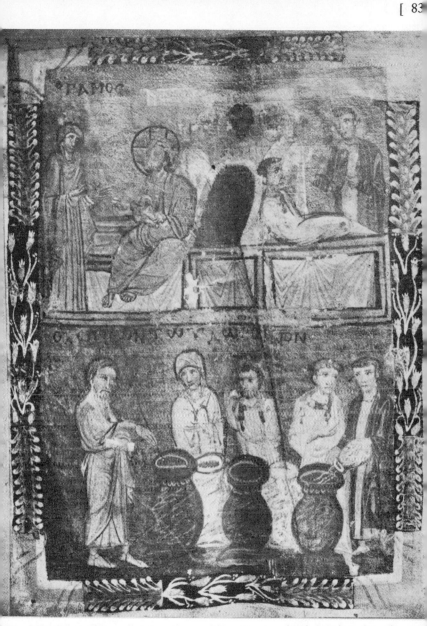

*The Miracle at Cana, showing the wedding feast and Christ changing the water
into wine: miniature of about 700 A.D. in a Greek lectionary in Leningr*
(Page 27)

Christ healing the man with the withered hand, and the two blind men on the road to Jericho.

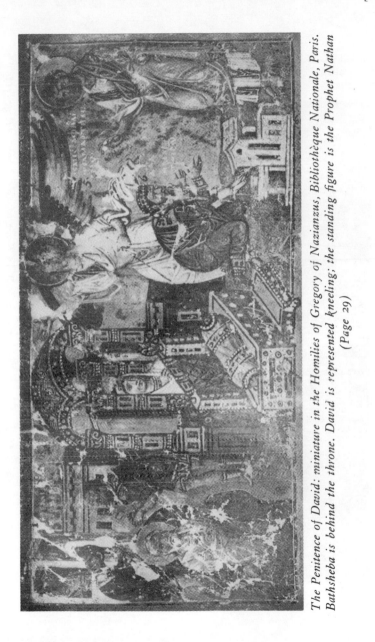

The Penitence of David: miniature in the Homilies of Gregory of Nazianzus, Bibliothèque Nationale, Paris. Bathsheba is behind the throne. David is represented kneeling; the standing figure is the Prophet Nathan

(Page 29)

The Harrowing of Hell: mosaic of about 1100 A.D. in Saint Mark's, Venice (Page 31)

Mary receiving from the High Priest the wool for the Veil of the Temple, scene from the apocryphal gospel of Saint James: mosaic of the fourteenth century in Kahrie Djami, Constantinople (Page 32)

Ravenna: S. Apollinare in Classe (Page 36)

Irish initial in the Book of Kells (Page 35)

*Scenes of the life and miracles of Christ on ivories of the
fifth century (Page 36)*

*Eighth century copies of the scenes
in plate on opposite page from an
ivory book cover in the Bodleian
Library at Oxford (Page 36)*

Utrecht Psalter: Nathan denouncing David's sin with Bathsheba; Uriah dead in battle; Parable of the Ewe-Lamb (Page 37)

Heaven and Hell and Saint Peter saving a soul;
English drawing, eleventh century (Page 38)

Moissac: Saint Peter (Page 41)

Nevers, Saint Etienne, nave (Page 43)

Creation of Man; of Woman; the Fall. Modena Cathedral: sculptures by Wiligelmus (Page 40)

Bronze Doors of Hildesheim; Christ before Pilate (Page 39)

Rome, Vatican Library, Museo Cristiano. Crucifixion, the Roman Wolf, the Madonna, Saints Gregory, Silvester, and Flavian. Ivory diptych dating circa 900 A.D. (Pages 36 and 40)

Amiens Cathedral: interior of nave (Page 49)

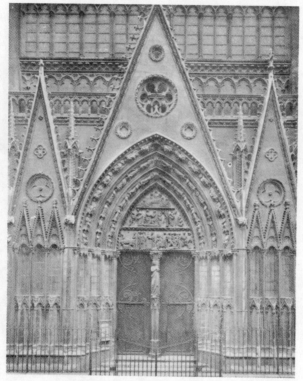

Paris, Notre Dame: north transept portal (Page 49)

Nevers Cathedral: pier capital (Page 48)

Rheims Cathedral: west façade (Page 50)

Giovanni Pisano: Madonna (Page 54)

*Bruges, Saint John's Hospital: the Madonna
of Martin Nieuwenhoven (Page 54)*

*Paris, Notre Dame: Madonna in the
choir; fourteenth century (Page 52)*

Ghent, Saint Bavon: the Adoration of the Lamb (Page 52)

New York, Morgan Library: page from the Windmill Psalter, English, fourteenth century. The scene above is the Judgment of Solomon; the initial is that of the first Psalm (Page 51)

Paris, Bibliothèque Nationale, Breviary of Belleville.
David before Saul; the dragonfly ("demoiselle," old
French "pucelle") on the left margin is the trade-mark
of the miniaturist Jean Pucelle (Page 51)

Cambridge, Fitz-William Museum, Pontifical of Metz.
The scene above is the dedication of a church, in
which the officiant traces the Greek alphabet (here
made into a border above the initial) on the pavement
(Page 51)

Hubert Van Eyck: the Birth of Saint John Baptist, and the Baptism of Christ, miniature from the "Hours of Milan" (Page 51)

Van Eyck: Madonna of Chancellor Rollin (Page 59)

Andrea del Sarto; Madonna of the Harpies (Page 60)

Filippo Lippi; Coronation of the Virgin, central portion
(Page 59)

J. Sansovino; Bacchus (Page 59)

Girardon; Rape of Proserpine (Page 66)

Michelangelo; Bound Slave (Page 62)

Bernini; Ecstasy of Saint Francis (Page 63)

Female Saint; Princeton Art Museum (Page 61)

Pedro de Mena; Saint Francis
(Page 66)

Rome; church of the Gesù, interior (Page 63)